batik &
tie dyeing

Cameron and Margaret Yerian, Editors

 CHILDRENS PRESS, CHICAGO

Executive Editors
Cameron John Yerian, M.A.
Margaret A. Yerian, M.A.

Art Director
Thomas Petiet, M.F.A.

Designer
Cameron John Yerian

Senior Editors
Mary Rush M.F.A.
Sharon Irvine, B.A.

Contributors
Nancy Muhlbach, M.A.
Jerry Gillmore, B.A.
Mary White, B.A.
Edith Wolter, B.S.
Susan Keezer
Barbara Daniel
Virginia Foster, A.B.

Editorial Assistant
Phoebe A. Yerian

Readability Consultants
Donald E.P. Smith, Ph.D.
School of Education
University of Michigan

Judith K. Smith, Ph.D.
University of Michigan

Instructional Development Consultant
Joel B. Fleming, M.A.
Instructional Development & Technology
Michigan State University

Synectics Consultant
Gershom Clark Morningstar, M.A.
President, Wolverine-Morningstar Media

Crafts Consultant
Laurie A. Flynn, B.A.
Little Seville Gallery, Pensacola, Fla.

Library Consultant
Noel Winkler, M.A.L.S.
Lecturer, Children's Literature
Elementary Librarian, Media Center
School of Education
University of Michigan

Library of Congress Cataloging in Publication Data

Yerian, Cameron John.
  Batik and tie dyeing.

  SUMMARY: Introduces basic techniques of tie dyeing,
batik, and dollmaking and suggests simple projects using
these techniques.
  "Fun time books."
  1. Batik—Juvenile literature. 2. Tie-dyeing—
Juvenile literature. 3. Dollmaking—Juvenile literature. [1. Batik. 2. Tie dyeing. 3. Dollmaking.
4. Handicraft] I. Yerian, Margaret, joint author.
II. Y^4 Design (Group of designers) III. Title.
TT852.5.Y47   746.6   74-8440
ISBN 0-516-01303-3

1 2 3 4 5 6 7 8 9 10 R 75 74

Contents

BATIK, TIE DYEING, PRETEND PEOPLE

Customize your clothes or your room. Make a colorful batik wall hanging. Tie dye your old shirts and jeans for a new, "with it" look. Construct delightful statues and dolls from old clothespins, dried apples, and cornhusks.

All these projects, and many more, are in this book. It's fun to make originals. Make things for yourself or your friends. Make things to sell or give as gifts.

Most of the projects can be made with very inexpensive materials. Some of them use things that you probably already have around the house, such as crayons, old rags or sheets, pieces of fabric, glue, or string.

These projects work. The pictures help you see each step. Most of the work you can do by yourself, but sometimes you may have to ask for help. If you can't do it alone, ask your older brother or sister, your parents, or your teacher to help.

Here are a few hints that make doing things safe and easy.

- Read the instructions carefully. Know where you are going.
- Get all the things you'll need *before* you start.
- Don't rush. "Practice makes perfect."
- Be CAREFUL. Don't burn or cut yourself.
- Don't make a mess. Clean up after yourself.

Let your creative self go! Remember you are the artist. Don't get discouraged. Every time you do a batik, or tie dye cloth, or make a cornhusk doll it will be different. The more you do the better you'll get.

HAVE FUN WITH THE FUN TIME BOOKS

Materials

BORROW your mother's muffin pan and a bigger cake pan.

SET the muffin pan inside the cake pan. Put these on a stove. An electric hot plate is even better.

PUT water in the cake pan. Heat it slowly. This works like your mother's double boiler. Keep water in it always as you work. Also keep an open box of baking soda handy in case of fire.

CUT a piece of wax into 1 inch squares. Sometimes this is called household paraffin. It is the kind used for canning.

PUT a square of wax in each muffin cup. Make sure the heat is low.

PEEL the paper off some crayons.

Put four red crayons in a cup with the wax. Let them melt slowly.

DON'T RUSH. You must be careful. Hot wax can burn badly.

PUT four crayons of the same color in a cup. Use bright colors—orange, yellow, blue, green, turquoise, magenta, yellow-green. You have room for twelve colors.

MELT these slowly.

GET several brushes. Use one for each color group. This helps to keep your colors clear and bright.

SPREAD newspapers on the table.

TAKE a piece of white cotton cloth. Ask your mother for an old sheet from her rag bag. Get something you can tear or cut.

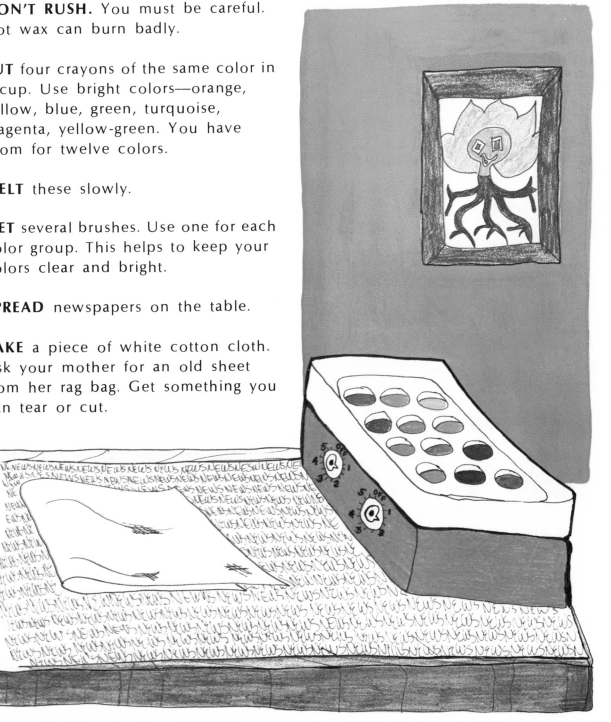

Now you are ready!

7

Club Flag

CUT a piece of white cotton cloth into a banner shape.

DRAW a design lightly in pencil on the cloth. Keep it simple. Big areas of color work best.

PAINT your design with the hot, colored wax. Use different brushes. Keep the waxes separate.

LEAVE small lines of white showing between colors.

MAKE SURE the wax soaks through the cloth. If it doesn't—turn the heat up a little. The wax needs to be hotter.

BE CAREFUL. There is no rush.

LET the wax dry on your cloth.

CRUMPLE the cloth in your hands gently. This gives the cracked look of batik.

MIX a strong batch of a dark-colored dye. Use hot water to mix it.

LET the dye cool.

PUT your cloth in the dye. The white areas will take the dye. The waxed areas will resist the dye.

LEAVE it in the dye for ten minutes. Then take it out.

LAY it on the newspapers to dry.

PUT paper towels on both sides of your flag. Then several layers of newspaper.

IRON it through the paper. Use medium heat. The papers will draw the wax from the cloth. The colors will stay.

USE more fresh paper. You may have to iron several times. Let it cool.

SEW a hem across the top of your flag.

PUT a dowel through the hem. Tie a bright piece of yarn to both ends.

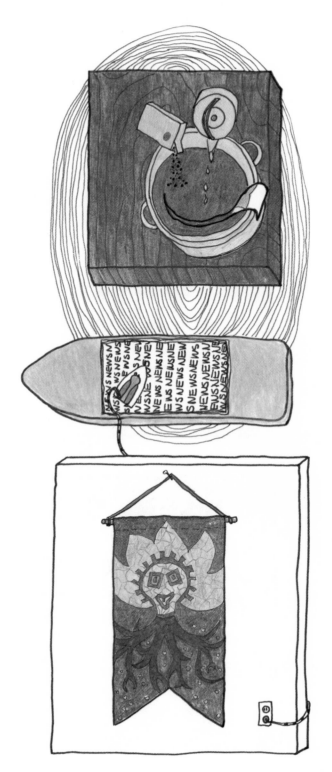

Booty Bag

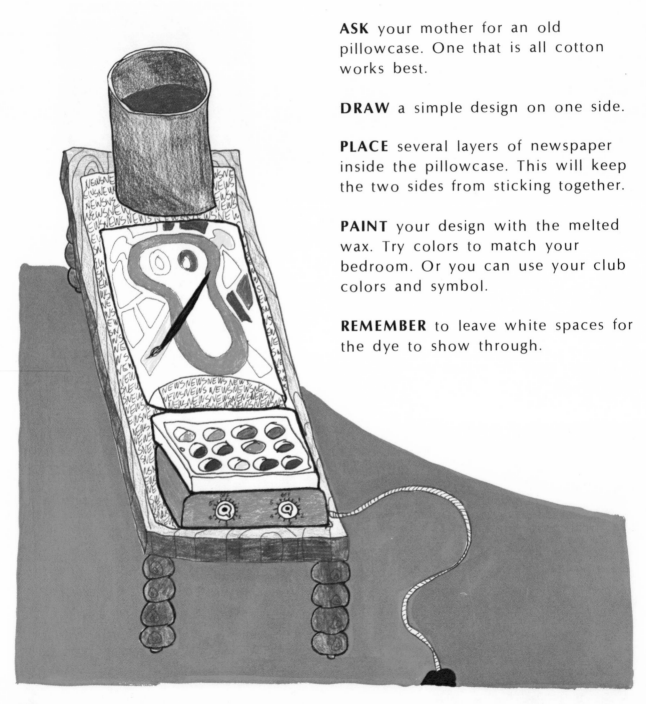

ASK your mother for an old pillowcase. One that is all cotton works best.

DRAW a simple design on one side.

PLACE several layers of newspaper inside the pillowcase. This will keep the two sides from sticking together.

PAINT your design with the melted wax. Try colors to match your bedroom. Or you can use your club colors and symbol.

REMEMBER to leave white spaces for the dye to show through.

MIX a strong dye batch. A color darker than the ones you have used so far will look best. A plastic tub works well for the dye.

LET your pillowcase soak in the dye for ten minutes.

TAKE it out and let it dry on newspapers.

PUT papers on both sides and iron it out.

MAKE SURE you get all the wax out.

PUT your pillowcase on your pillow for decoration. Throw it on your bed. It can also hold your pajamas. Or, if you used your club symbol, you have a booty bag.

Batik Frame

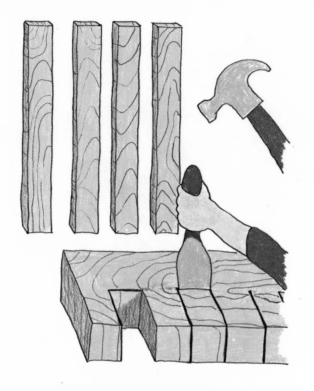

USE an old picture frame if you have one. If not. . .

GET four pieces of 1 by 2 inch pine wood. They should be the same length.

MAKE two saw cuts 1 inch into the wide side of the wood. Make them 1-1/8 inch apart.

MEASURE carefully. Do this the same distance from the end of each piece of wood.

USE a hammer and chisel to knock out the wood between the cuts. Give it a good knock.

FIT the slots together into a frame.

CUT other slots in your frame, if you wish. Then you can make it many sizes.

REMEMBER to measure each cut. Also make the cuts in the same place on each piece of wood.

PIN your cloth to the frame. Use push pins or thumb tacks. This will make the cloth easier to paint. The wax will soak through better.

Place Mats

TEAR six pieces of cotton cloth about 12 by 18 inches. You can do more if you like. Just make them the same size.

DRAW a simple design in pencil.

PICK colors to match your mother's dishes.

PAINT the design on the cloth with the melted wax. Even if the design is the same, each mat will be a little different.

LET the wax dry, then crackle it.

DYE each place mat. Then let them dry on newspapers.

IRON each one out carefully.

PULL a few threads gently on each edge. This will make a fringe.

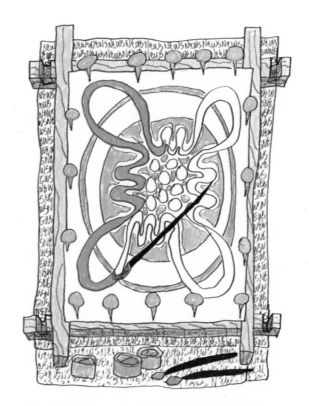

You can also make plain colored napkins. Choose a color that is in your design. This could make a nice gift.

Printing with Wax

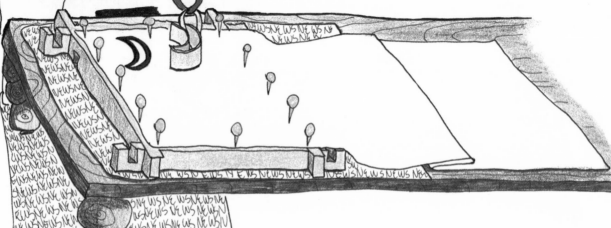

ASK your mother for an old sheet.

TEAR a long strip about 2 feet wide. Make it long enough to fit the length of your dining room table—or a picnic table. This is called a runner.

TAKE 2 metal cookie cutters.

GET a pair of pliers. Use them to hold the cookie cutter. It will get hot.

DIP the first cookie cutter into the wax. Hold it there for at least 25 seconds.

SHAKE off extra wax carefully.

STAMP the cookie cutter along the edge of the runner.

TAKE the second cookie cutter with the pliers.

DIP it in a different color and repeat.

KEEP changing back and forth. One cutter and that color, then the other cutter and its color. Repeat this until the end of the runner.

DO this on the other edge of the runner also.

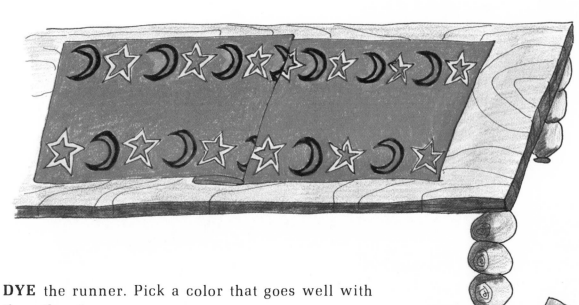

DYE the runner. Pick a color that goes well with the other two.

IRON it out after it is dry. Keep changing to clean papers as you iron.

You can make runners for different holidays and special times.

PLAN a picnic and invite your friends.

USE one of your runners on the table. Show them some of your other projects.

Perhaps they would like to try batik. Not too many kids at a time, though!

TIE
dyEiNG

Materials

GATHER two big pans or buckets, a stirring stick, old newspapers, lots of rubber bands, dye, and cotton cloth.

FIND a good place to work because this will make a mess. Put newspaper on the floor. Arrange a place to dry your cloth. Wear old clothes.

FILL one pan with warm water, and fill another pan with very hot water. Put both pans on the newspaper.

POUR some dye into the very hot water, and stir it with your stick. Try not to put your hands in the dye because the color will not wash off.

RIP your cloth to the size you want. Wet it in the clear water. Squeeze out the water.

18

Silly Circles

PICK a spot on your wet cloth to be the middle of your circle.

BUNCH the cloth together.

PUT a rubber band around the cloth. Lots of rubber bands can be put on. Make sure that all of the rubber bands are tight. You can make one big circle or lots of small ones.

PUT the cloth into the dye. Stir the water until your cloth is a little darker than you want it. Use the stick to take the cloth out of the dye.

RINSE the cloth in your bucket of clear water. Get new water if you need to.

PUT the cloth in a good drying place until it is dry. The color will fade if you put it in the sun or try to hurry with an iron.

TAKE OFF the rubber bands.

SEW a hem all around your cloth. Now you have a tablecloth.

Strange Shapes

SCROUNGE lots of small things. They can be stones, seeds, beans, buttons, and other small things. Make sure that they are clean and that no one will need them again.

ASK your mother for an old pillowcase.

PUT your wet pillowcase flat on the floor or on a table. Put one of your small things inside the pillowcase and bunch the cloth around it. Wrap a rubber band around the cloth and make sure it is tight. You can do this on both sides. If it is hard to put on a rubber band, try tying on string.

ADD many more things to your cloth and wrap a rubber band around each one.

PLACE your pillowcase in the dye. Dye it just as you dyed the circles.

When it is dry, you will have your own special TV pillow cover.

Fine Lines

PUT another wet pillowcase flat on the floor or on a table.

BEGIN at one end and start making folds in the cloth.

FOLD all of the cloth, then it is ready for rubber bands. Put lots of rubber bands around your cloth. Make sure that they are tight.

PUT the cloth into the dye. Dye it as before. Let it dry.

EXPERIMENT folding cloth different ways. You can make folds in both directions. Or you can fold the cloth into triangles.

When this pillowcase is done, you will have two. Now you can have a bright stuff bag.

Many Colors

GET several dye colors and a big pan or bucket for each color. Yellow, blue, and red are good colors.

FILL each bucket with very hot water, and pour one color into each bucket. Stir the dye just as you did before.

PREPARE some cloth for the dyes. Make circles, lines, or strange shapes.

START with the lightest color first and dip part of the cloth into the dye. Squeeze out the dye water gently and dye another part of the cloth in the next darkest dye. Keep working until all of the cloth has been dyed.

RINSE and dry your cloth just as you did before.

EXPERIMENT with other pieces of cloth. You can make three colors on your cloth with only two buckets of dye.

MAKE circles, strange shapes, and lines on the same piece of cloth. Use two or three dye colors.

Tie Dye Collage

GATHER scissors, glue, and something for the back of your collage. Burlap or cardboard work well. Save several pieces of tie-dyed cloth.

CUT OUT pieces of tie-dyed cloth. Try to find interesting designs in different colors and sizes.

PLACE the pieces of cloth on your burlap or cardboard. Move them around until the pattern pleases you.

GLUE the pieces of cloth into place.

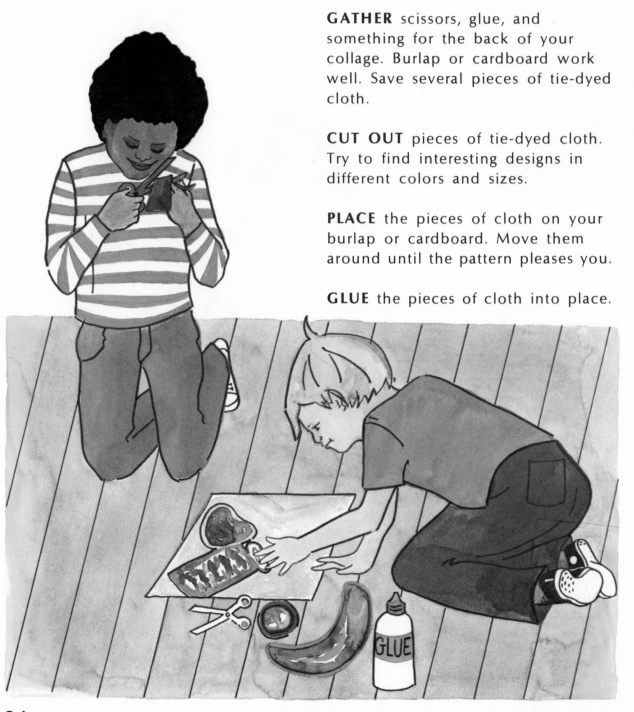

Tie Dye Mobile

GATHER scissors, glue, thread, colored paper, and a good stick or coat hanger. Save pieces of tie-dyed cloth.

CUT your tie-dyed cloth into interesting shapes.

GLUE the shapes onto colored paper, and cut the paper around the shape.

POKE a hole in each shape and tie on some thread.

TIE each thread onto your stick or coat hanger. Glue the thread in place so that it won't slip.

A Big Project

TRY something really big.

ASK your mother for an old cotton sheet. You could sew some small pieces of cloth together to make a big piece.

INVITE a friend to help. This will be a big job.

THINK of all the great things that you can use your tie-dyed sheet for.

You could make a bedspread.

You could use it as a stage curtain.

It could even be a tent.

What else could it be!

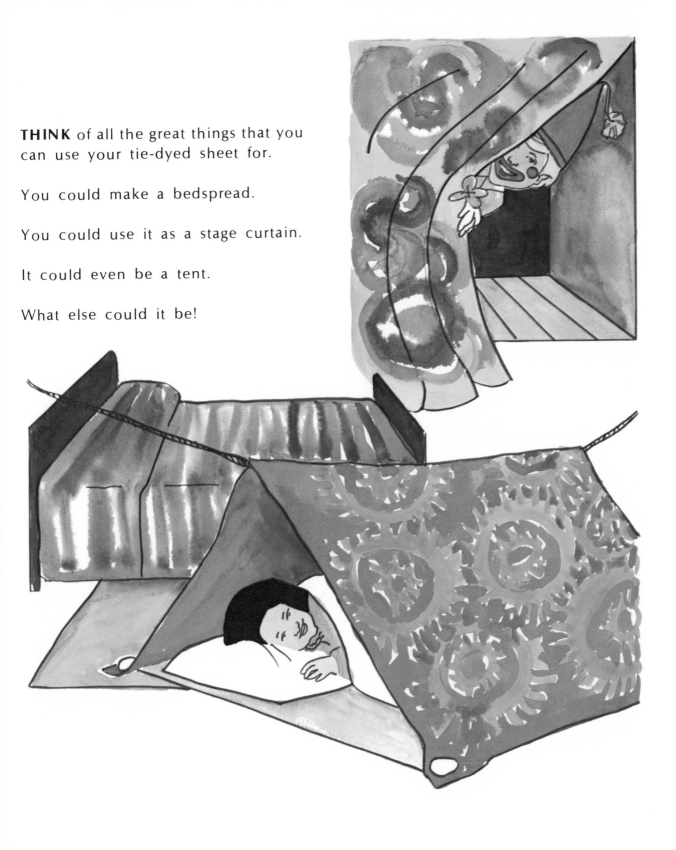

Ugly Shirt Contest

GET scissors, glue, paper, and ribbon. Make awards for the contest. They can be for the ugliest, most colorful, or the silliest shirts. Try to think of your own awards.

COLLECT your friends and ask each one to bring a cotton shirt. Arrange a work place as you did before, but have lots more rubber bands and a bigger place to dry the tie-dyed cloth. Mix several dyes in very hot water.

WET your shirt and squeeze out the water. Make line and circle patterns all over it. The rubber bands must be tight. Help your friends who have never done tie dye.

DIP part of your shirt into the lightest dye. Stir it, but try not to splash on your hands or on the rest of the shirt. Carefully squeeze out the dye and dip another part of the shirt into the next dye. Keep working until the whole shirt is dyed the way you want it.

RINSE your shirt in clear water and hang it to dry. Help your friends until everyone has dyed a shirt.

WAIT until the shirts are dry. Help the time to pass by cleaning up your mess.

REMOVE the rubber bands and open up your shirt. Ask an adult to judge the shirts and pin the awards on the winners.

PRETEND PEOPLE

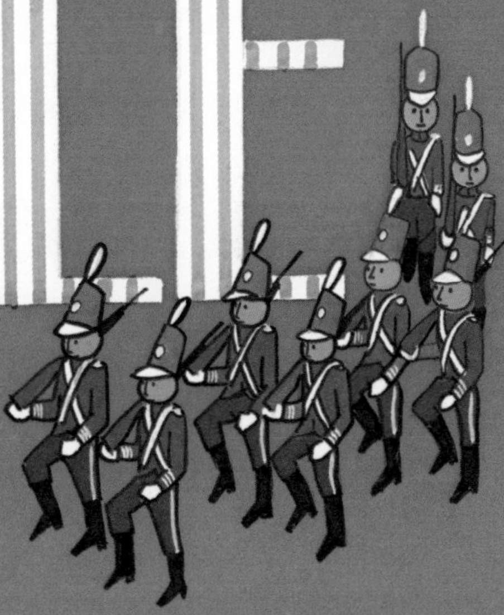

Kings & Things

COLLECT some empty thread or wire spools, wooden dresser knobs, and caps from plastic bottles.

GET some straws, old clothespins, or any other small things that look fun.

GLUE the spools, knobs, and bottle caps together with white glue. Make them look like kings, drummers, flag bearers or any kind of interesting people you can think of.

PAINT the people with bright colors. Put stripes, crosses, or squiggles on their clothes.

USE any materials you think will make them interesting. Give the people armor, flags, swords, or whatever you want.

Clothespin People

GET some plain wooden clothespins.

SAND the bottoms of the clothespins until they are flat and will stand alone.

GIVE the clothespins bodies and faces with paint or felt pens.

CUT some clothes from felt scraps if you want. Glue them onto your people when the paint is dry.

MAKE them look like people or monsters or whatever is fun for you.

GLUE your clothespin people onto a board if you would like them to hold your papers.

PUT them on the board in pairs. Make sure they are across from each other.

DAB some white glue on the feet and hold them on the board until they begin to dry. Put your papers between each pair of people.

Applehead People

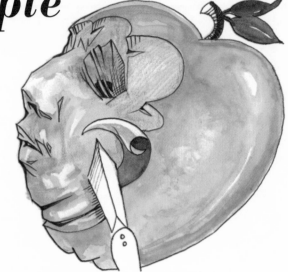

GET a medium sized greenish apple.

PEEL the apple carefully. Keep it as smooth as you can. Take a little of the core out of the bottom.

CARVE a face on one side of the apple. Use a small knife. Cut the eyes in quite deeply and let the nose stick out.

GIVE the apple a mouth and ears. Carve away little bits of the apple around parts of the face that you want to stick out.

RUN your fingernail along the forehead and cheeks if you want wrinkles.

SOAK the apple for ten minutes in lemon juice. Push a pencil into the place where you took out the core.

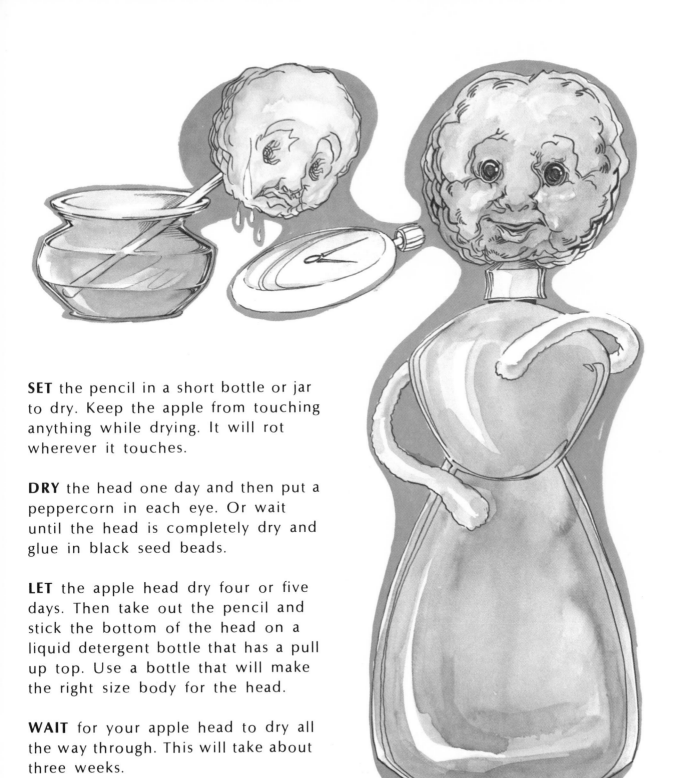

SET the pencil in a short bottle or jar to dry. Keep the apple from touching anything while drying. It will rot wherever it touches.

DRY the head one day and then put a peppercorn in each eye. Or wait until the head is completely dry and glue in black seed beads.

LET the apple head dry four or five days. Then take out the pencil and stick the bottom of the head on a liquid detergent bottle that has a pull up top. Use a bottle that will make the right size body for the head.

WAIT for your apple head to dry all the way through. This will take about three weeks.

Finishing Touches

MAKE arms for your person from two pipe cleaners. Twist them together and glue them across the back of the bottle. Add some tape if you have trouble making the arms stick.

BEND the arms down and put on clay hands. Use the kind of clay that dries hard. Shape it into little wads and stick it on the ends of the pipe cleaner arms.

DAB some paint on the cheeks to give the face a little more color if you like.

GLUE cotton on the head for hair. Or use some other material that looks like hair to you.

MAKE clothes for your apple head person from felt, leather, or fabric scraps. Glue them to the bottle body.

DRESS your person like an Eskimo, an Indian, an old lady with a long dress, or anything else you like.

GIVE your person a hat, glasses, a bow and arrow, flowers, or whatever is right for the kind of person you made.

Vegetable People

MAKE some silly people from carrots, potatoes, or other solid vegetables.

CHOOSE odd shapes that make you think of people. If you use a separate piece for the head, hold it on the body by pushing a round toothpick through both pieces.

MAKE arms from pipe cleaners or round toothpicks. Put in toothpick legs. Cut a cork in half for feet or use two potato slices.

PUT a face on your person. You can cut it from felt or paper and glue it on. You can paint it on. Or you can glue on little things.

TRY beads or thumbtacks for eyes. Use a piece of cotton for a round nose. Make a long, pointed nose with a paper cone or the small end of a carrot.

GIVE your people hats, scarves, glasses, a mustache, or whatever you want.

Spinning People

KEEP a large, empty wooden spool.

GET a piece of 1/8 inch dowel, two wooden beads with large holes, and some felt scraps.

DRAW a line around the middle of the spool.

USE a coping saw to cut the spool on the line. One spool will make two people.

SAND the cut ends of the spool until they are smooth.

CUT a 2-1/4 inch piece of dowel for each half of the spool. Sand one end until it is a point with a flat end.

PAINT clothes on the pieces of spool and faces on the beads. Make them silly or scary. Put the end of a pencil in the holes to hold them while you paint.

WRAP a little masking tape around the dowel. Put it about 1/2 inch from the pointed end.

DAB some glue on the tape and push the dowel into the hole in the spool. The flat end of the dowel should be a little above the part of the spool that you cut.

CUT a round circle from the felt scraps. Use it for a collar. Cut a hole in the middle of the circle and slip it over the top of the dowel.

GLUE the bead head on top of the dowel. Hold the head on the collar until the glue dries.

SPIN your people around like a top. Have spinning races or make them dance.

TAPE

Cornhusk People

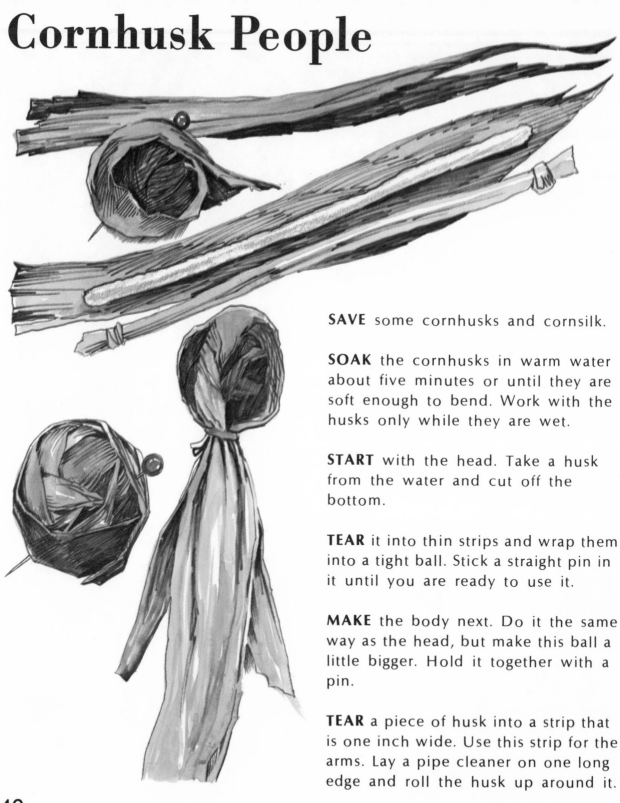

SAVE some cornhusks and cornsilk.

SOAK the cornhusks in warm water about five minutes or until they are soft enough to bend. Work with the husks only while they are wet.

START with the head. Take a husk from the water and cut off the bottom.

TEAR it into thin strips and wrap them into a tight ball. Stick a straight pin in it until you are ready to use it.

MAKE the body next. Do it the same way as the head, but make this ball a little bigger. Hold it together with a pin.

TEAR a piece of husk into a strip that is one inch wide. Use this strip for the arms. Lay a pipe cleaner on one long edge and roll the husk up around it.

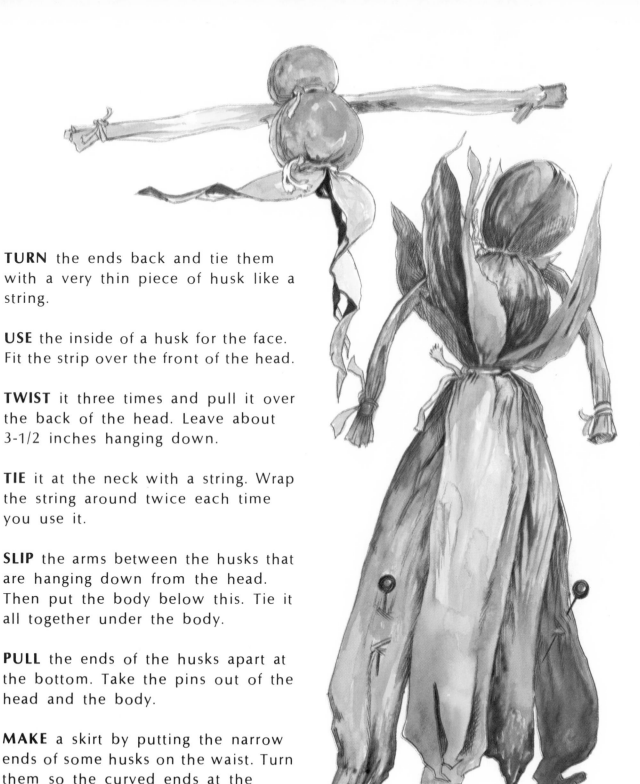

TURN the ends back and tie them with a very thin piece of husk like a string.

USE the inside of a husk for the face. Fit the strip over the front of the head.

TWIST it three times and pull it over the back of the head. Leave about 3-1/2 inches hanging down.

TIE it at the neck with a string. Wrap the string around twice each time you use it.

SLIP the arms between the husks that are hanging down from the head. Then put the body below this. Tie it all together under the body.

PULL the ends of the husks apart at the bottom. Take the pins out of the head and the body.

MAKE a skirt by putting the narrow ends of some husks on the waist. Turn them so the curved ends at the bottom point in.

41

KEEP adding more husks until your lady can stand alone. Tie a string at the waist to hold the husks.

TRIM the ends of the cornhusks off at the waist so only a little sticks up above the string.

MEASURE 5-1/2 inches below the waist. Trim the cornhusks off here to make the skirt even all the way around.

SPREAD one cornhusk out over another all the way around the skirt. Pin them together. Leave the pins in until the lady is finished and the cornhusks are dry.

MAKE a blouse by first tearing a husk down the middle the long way.

HOLD the husk at the left side of the waist and put it over the right shoulder. Put the other piece of husk on the opposite way so that the husks cross in the front and in the back.

TIE a narrow strip of husk around the waist to hold the blouse on.

SOAK some cornsilk in warm water for the hair. Then wrap it around the head in any hair style you want.

SEW the hair to the head with a needle and brown thread.

GIVE your lady some kind of head covering if you like.

MAKE a head scarf from a piece of husk that is tied under her chin. Tie three pieces of husk together and braid them for a headband. Or sew some braids together to make a hat.

USE cornhusks, broom bristles, and a pipe cleaner if you want to make a broom. Tie them together with a thin piece of husk and sew the broom to the hands.

PUT some tissue paper under the skirt. Let your lady stand overnight in a dry place.

USE your ideas and see what kind of lady you can make

43

Pretend People Hunt

DECIDE on a time and place for your hunt. Make a person ahead of time and keep it a secret. Bring the pretend person to the hunt in a sack.

MAKE a slip of paper for everyone who will be at the hunt. Write the name of a hiding place on each slip. Have a free area where there are no hiding places.

FOLD the slips and put them in a box. Mix them up so no one knows what they say.

HAVE each friend take a slip when he comes in. One friend at a time should go to the hiding place named on his slip and hide his pretend person there. Everyone else must stay in the free area.

GIVE everyone a piece of paper and tell them to write down five clues about their person and where it is hidden. Mix these papers up in a box and let everyone draw one. Put the slip back and try again if you get your own.

TRY to find the pretend person on your paper by using the clues. Then see if you can guess who it belongs to. See how many pretend people can be found in 15 minutes.

INDEX

ILLUSTRATORS

INSTANT BATIK
page   5: Thomas Petiet
page   6-16: Susan H. Frens

TIE DYEING
page   17: Thomas Petiet
page   18-30: Elizabeth Golz Rush

PRETEND PEOPLE
page   31: Thomas Petiet
page   32-44: David LaVerne Laetz

About the Editors

Cameron John and Margaret A. Yerian have advanced degrees in psychology and mass communications from the University of Michigan. They have been active in educational and instructional writing for both adults and children, with many publications to their credit. Their work has ranged from the Educational Television Project in American Samoa, where Mrs. Yerian served as a producer/director and Mr. Yerian was a writer and editor to their present work as media consultants in the Detroit metropolitan area.